# Digital Animation for Kids

## *Bring Your Stories to Life*

# Table of Contents

# Chapter 1. Introduction

Welcome to our Special Report: "Digital Animation for Kids: Bring Your Stories to Life!" This is no ordinary guide, but rather an enchanting look into the magical world of digital animation, ideal for sparking creativity in your young ones. We promise not just technicalities, but an exciting adventure that unveils the possibility of turning those bedtime storytelling sessions into vivid, animated masterpieces. You'll uncover charming tips and tricks, experience interesting and accessible tutorials, and unearth the secrets of making thoughts come alive in dazzling colors. Ready to join this extraordinary journey? This special report has the power to encourage, inspire, and transform curious learners into young creators, making it a delightful and worthy addition to your home library. So, let's prepare to turn possible into reality and your child's ideas into inspiring animations!

# Chapter 2. Introduction to Digital Animation

Digital animation is transforming the means, modes, and methods of storytelling among children. Imagine, instead of solely verbalizing stories for your children at bedtime, you visually illustrate the tales by bringing characters to life. The dragons breathing fire, the princess fleeing the tower, the world below a rabbit's hole, all convalescing into a sequence of animation. That, in its essence, is the magic and appeal of digital animation. In this chapter, we journey into understanding this enchanting medium, which amalgamates technology with imagination.

## 2.1. Digital animation: An Overview

Digital animation, at its core, is the art of creating moving images via the use of digital technology. It has considerably democratized the animation space, letting even those without a traditional art background create dynamic stories with characters that seem to leap off the screen. It diversifies storytelling by adding a visual and interactive facet to it. With a computer, software, and bit of practice, kids can convert their delightful stories into engaging animations.

The digital art space is not all about full-length animated movies. While Pixar or DreamWorks may tickle your thoughts, remember that even a simple blinking light or a jumping ball is part of digital animation. The scope is vast, and it's up to the young animator to determine how simple or complex they want their digital creation to be.

## 2.2. The Basics: Frames, Storyboarding, and Animation Techniques

A fundamental concept in digital animation is the understanding of Frames. If you flip through the pages of a book rapidly, the illusion of movement is created. Similarly, animation works using a consecutive string of static images, or frames. A typical animation video consists of 24 frames each second on the screen. With more frames per second (fps), the video's motion becomes smoother and more realistic.

Storyboarding is another essential part of the animation planning process. It's a visual representation, almost like a comic strip, of what the animation will look like. Here, the focus is not on detailed artwork but rather on presenting the sequence of events and ensuring the story flows logically.

There are two main methods of making digital animation - 2D (two dimensions) and 3D (three dimensions). 2D animation is flat and only has height and width, like a drawing on a piece of paper. In contrast, 3D animation adds depth to the mix, making the characters and scenarios look more realistic.

## 2.3. Tools of the Trade: Useful Software

Digital animation thrives on the efficiency and capabilities provided by software tools. While some of these can lean on the expensive side, many offer free versions that are excellent for children starting their animation journey. These include Tux Paint, Pencil 2D, and Blender. Each of these software tools have their strengths, and using them can be an adventure of its own.

## 2.4. Getting Started with Your First Animation

Digital animation for beginners need not be daunting, even if it sounds like a massive task. The first step is always the easiest - just start! Think of a simple object and try to animate it on one of the software tools. Starting with something as simple as animating a bouncing ball is a great way to learn the ropes.

## 2.5. The Journey Beyond: Developing Skills and Finding Inspiration

Now that the basics have been covered, the next steps are mastering complex techniques and staying inspired. Animate objects of varying shapes, work on creating smooth transitions, experiment with the color palette, and watch a lot of animation! Animation is a skill that improves with practice and patience. These explorations will provide a foundation that your child can use to tell their stories, be they traditional fairy tales or wild space adventures.

The adventure of digital animation does not end with mastering the software. It is a medium that thrives on the brilliance of imagination. Inspire your child to explore the vast territories of their creativity with the power of digital animation. It's not just about bringing stories to life, but about allowing them to create their worlds - with their rules, characters, and magic.

In this chapter, we touched the surface of digital animation, imagining what we can achieve. From understanding what frames are, to beginning your first animation, we now have a solid foothold to begin our creative expedition. The next chapters will guide you further into the magical forest of digital animation, exploring techniques, tools, and creativity. So, let us continue on our quest, turning ideas and thoughts into vivid and enchanting animations.

# Chapter 3. The Tools of the Trade: Software and Hardware Essentials

To set the stage for the drawn magic and create an animated universe, there are certain essential tools and pieces of equipment that are required. These include various types of software and hardware. We are about to dive into that world now!

## 3.1. Software Essentials

When it comes to animation software, there are many options available. We will explore a few popular ones here, detailing their features, ease of use, and any costs involved. This tour is designed to help you choose what's best for your child.

1. **Toon Boom Harmony**: Frequently used in professional studios, Toon Boom Harmony is a versatile software that can cater to simple and complex projects alike. It's great for teaching different animation techniques, like keyframing, traditional paper animation, cut-out, and more. It can be a bit complex for beginners, but has adaptable tools suitable for different experience levels.

2. **Adobe Anime (Previously Adobe Flash)**: This software offers a user-friendly interface making it good for beginners. It's perfect for creating web-based animations. With its extensive tools, you can create great motion graphics and visual effects.

3. **Pencil2D**: For beginners who are testing waters in the animation world, Pencil2D could be a great starting point. It is free and open-source with features that are easy to understand. It enables creating 2D hand-drawn animations.

4. **Blender**: A powerful, and free, open-source 3D creation suite that supports all aspects of 3D development. It includes 3D modeling, rigging, animation, simulation, rendering, compositing and tracking, motion tracking, and even video editing.

5. **Clip Studio Paint**: Originally designed for manga artists, Clip Studio Paint is increasingly gaining popularity in the animation arena. It's great for frame-by-frame animation and is lauded for its natural drawing feel.

# 3.2. Hardware Essentials

Now that we have covered software, let's move onto hardware. While software is the brains, hardware is the body. It's what you use to interact with the software and bring your visions to life.

1. **Computer**: A computer is a must, whether desktop or laptop. Its performance substantially affects the quality and speed of your work. Look for a computer with a powerful processor, enough RAM (16GB or more is recommended), a solid state drive for faster data access, and a good quality graphic card for better rendering.

2. **Drawing Tablet**: To create detailed animations, a drawing tablet is an essential tool. It allows you to draw directly into your computer, which results in natural and smooth strokes. Wacom tablets are often recommended, but Huion and XP-Pen are also brands that make high-quality tablets at a more affordable price.

3. **Scanner**: If your child enjoys drawing on paper, a scanner will be useful to digitalize these drawings for further processing in the animation software.

4. **Lightbox or Lightpad**: This tool is handy for traditional paper animation (used with animation paper). It ensures even light distribution, making it easier to see drawn frames when they are layered upon one another for creating animations.

5. **Animation Stand**: In stop-motion animation, an animation stand provides the stable platform to set your stage and scenes keeping the camera steadiness.

# 3.3. Software in Detail

Let's dig deeper into each piece of software and learn more about its unique features, so you can choose the one most suitable for your child.

## 3.3.1. Toon Boom Harmony

Toon Boom Harmony is known for its superior flexibility. Used by small animation studios as well as big names like Disney and Pixar, it offers a wide range of tools and features.

It allows for various animation styles such as paperless (most common), paper animation, cut-out animation, and even a combination of these styles. This flexibility makes it an excellent platform for fostering creativity and developing a wide range of skills.

## 3.3.2. Adobe Animate

Previously known as Adobe Flash, Adobe Animate is a comprehensive platform perfect for interactive and animated web content. This makes it excellent for creating online games and adverts, but it is also an incredible tool for storyboarding and 2D animation.

Its intuitive interface and beginner-friendly toolset make it a good starting point for youngsters who are new to animation. Plus, since Adobe produces it, there's a wealth of tutorials and resources available online.

### 3.3.3. Pencil2D

This minimalist open-source software is an excellent starting point for kids due to its simplicity. It's a 2D animation software that seamlessly combines bitmap and vector graphics.

Its easy-to-use set-up doesn't overwhelm beginners with a complex assortment of tools. Instead, it lets them focus on their creativity and gradually learn the ropes of the world of animation.

### 3.3.4. Blender

Blender, a 3D animation software, is a free and open-source tool loved by many pros and beginners. As a comprehensive suite, it allows for modeling, rigging, animation, simulation, rendering, compositing, and motion tracking, apart from video editing and game creation features.

Despite its professional-grade capabilities, Blender's user-friendly interface makes it accessible for young creators. It is especially renowned for its strong and dedicated community, offering ample tutorials and assistance for those new to 3D.

### 3.3.5. Clip Studio Paint

Clip Studio Paint is highly popular among manga and comic artists but has impressive animation capabilities too. Its particular strength lies in capturing the nuanced shading and texturing of hand-drawn work, bringing an authentic and natural feeling to digital animation.

Its relatively low price point, coupled with its convincing brush engine and comfortable user interface, makes it a strong contender for young artists wanting a smooth transition from traditional drawing to digital work.

# 3.4. Hardware in Detail

Each hardware component plays a crucial role in your animation journey. Here's what each element brings to the table.

## 3.4.1. Computer

Every application and command you use in the animation process gets processed through the computer; hence, having a robust system is vital.

While choosing a system, prioritize a fast processor, as that would process every command swiftly. Choose a computer with plenty of memory, which will allow it to handle large files smoothly. Consider a system with quality graphics hardware, as it will provide a better visual experience.

## 3.4.2. Drawing Tablet

Drawing tablets help in creating accurate and natural-looking strokes. They come with pressure sensitivity levels, allowing lighter or heavier strokes based on how much pressure you apply.

Brands such as Wacom, Huion, and XP-Pen offer a range of tablets from beginner to professional. Investing in a tablet with a screen like the Wacom Cintiq models can significantly boost the animation experience, but even without a screen, tablets provide improved control compared with a mouse.

## 3.4.3. Scanner

Scanners help bring traditional hand-drawn art to the digital world. High-quality scanners can capture these art pieces' nuanced details, preserving the soul of the original work.

A scanner might not be as critical if your child fully embraces digital creation, but it can be handy if they enjoy a blend of traditional and digital techniques.

### 3.4.4. Lightbox or Lightpad

For animations done on paper, a lightbox or lightpad becomes indispensable. It simplifies the process of tracing over the previous frame and hence, saves up on time and effort. It also allows for more precise drawings.

### 3.4.5. Animation Stand

In stop-motion animation, an animation stand provides a steady base to set up the scenes and helps maintain the camera's steady placement.

Your chosen software and hardware tools set the foundation for the animation journey. You don't need to get everything at once - start with the basics and upgrade as skills improve. Essential, though, is to foster a learning environment that encourages curiosity, creativity, and the joy of making imaginations come alive. The magic of animation truly lies there.

# Chapter 4. Understanding the Basics: From Sketch to Screen

Let's start at the very foreground of animation, where every legendary animator begins, with a simple sketch. The transformation from a sketch, an initial idea on paper, to a moving, living character on your screen, may seem like magic. But it's not. It's a combination of creativity, technical skills, and a good intuitive understanding of how motion works. Once you break it down into its basic steps, you'll see that it's something anyone passionate enough can learn.

## 4.1. Understanding Sketching

The first step in any animation is creating an initial sketch of what you will animate. Sketching helps to get your ideas onto paper and makes it easier to visualize your final result. Using simple geometric shapes and lines, come up with a basic outline of your character or scene.

All drawings begin as lines and shapes - circles, squares, triangles. A head might be a circle with two smaller circles for eyes and a triangle for the nose. Think of your characters and animation in these terms and it will vastly simplify the process. Try to pick characters which are not too complex at first. As you get familiar with shapes, you can move on to more complex designs.

Take a piece of paper and start drawing a character using simple shapes. Practice this till you're comfortable with creating shapes that resemble the character you have in mind.

## 4.2. Bringing the Sketches to Life

With a basic understanding of sketching characters and settings, you have the foundation required for animation. The next step is to bring your drawings to life.

An animation is simply a sequence of drawings, slightly changed from one to the other, that when viewed in rapid succession, gives the illusion of movement. This is known as the "frame-by-frame" technique.

Break down the character's movement into frames. Each frame is a drawing on its own. There is a starting and ending frame, with in-between frames depicting the transition.

For example, if you want to animate a character waving, you might start with one frame where the character's hand is at their side (starting frame), then a frame where the hand is halfway up (in-between frame), and finally one where the hand is fully raised (ending frame).

Once you have these "keyframes," you fill in the motion in between with additional frames. These frames are called "in-betweens." The more in-between frames you have, the smoother the motion will appear.

# 4.3. Understanding Software for Animation

Now that you understand the basic concept of animation, you need a platform to work on. Several digital animation software tools are out there that are easy to learn and ideal for kids. Some of these include FlipaClip, Toon Boom Harmony, and Adobe Animate CC. Look for software that is user-friendly and comes with tutorials to help beginners navigate through it.

As you get started with the chosen software, some features to explore include the drawing tools, frame-by-frame editor, layers, camera effects, and the exporting options.

## 4.4. Indoctrination into Digital Tools

Once you have chosen an animation software, you will first need to import your sketches and break them down into individual parts that can be manipulated. Most software allows scanning and uploading your sketches, or directly drawing in the software using a drawing tablet or a mouse.

Layers in animation software work much like they do in paper animation or cell animation. They allow you to separate parts of your animation to work on individually without affecting the rest. Each part of your scene or character that you animate separately should be on its own layer.

The frame-by-frame timeline is where you will spend most of your time, modifying your sketches and adding keyframes and in-betweens.

Camera effects are key in giving your animation a professional-looking finish. They allow you to zoom, pan, tilt, and rotate your scene to give it depth and movement.

Exporting options are necessary for sharing your final animations. Most software tools allow export in MP4 format, which can be easily shared and viewed on most devices.

## 4.5. Lessons on Motion and Timing

In successions of subtly-changing images, the brain perceives motion. It is here that we run into a crucial factor: timing. Timing is vital in defining speed and rhythm of the animated sequences. If the frames change rapidly, your character will seem to move faster. On the other hand, slower changes will make the character appear slower.

Understanding timing in animation is understanding that it gives your character "life". It translates the weight, mood, and personality of your characters into visual terms.

# 4.6. Practice

The final step, and arguably the most important, is consistent practice. The art of animation requires continuous learning and development of skill over time. With determination and patience, your child can master the basics and gradually take on more complex projects.

Remember that everyone learns at their own pace and it's okay to make mistakes. What matters most is that your child is encouraged to be creative, explore, and have fun!

# 4.7. Wrapping Up

With a good comprehension of sketching, the frame-by-frame technique, digital tools, and motion principles, you and your child are now prepared to embark on the magical journey of animation. Whether it's for a school project or simply creating stories from imagination, the skills acquired from understanding these basics will prove invaluable.

Bring those doodles and characters in the margins of notebooks to life, let your child's imagination run free. And always remember, animation is not just about creating movement, it's about telling stories. So, get those sketch pads ready, download an animation software, and start creating your first animated story!

# Chapter 5. The Power of Colors: Choosing the Right Palette

Color is a critical element in animation, determining the mood, the feel, and the story's tone. It influences the audience's emotional response and guides their connection with the characters and the story. Carefully chosen colors can transform a simple scene into a powerful, emotionally influential masterpiece.

## 5.1. Understanding Color Theory

Every enlightening journey into the world of colors begins with the fundamentals of color theory. Color theory is a framework that guides us on how to utilize, mix, and relate different colors. At its core is the color wheel, containing primary (red, blue, and yellow), secondary (green, orange, and violet), and tertiary colors (the result of mixing a primary color with a secondary color).

Further detailing this concept, each color is associated with specific emotions and reactions. Warm colors like red, yellow, and orange bring feelings of warmth and comfort but also feelings of anger and hostility. Cool colors, such as green, blue, and purple, often incite feelings of calm and sadness.

Once familiar with these concepts, you can play around and consult the color wheel to form a color scheme—to create harmony or contrast in your animation scenes. Typical color schemes include:

- Monochromatic: This scheme uses different shades, tints, and tones within the same color family. It brings a sense of visual cohesion and can communicate a specific mood or emotion effectively.

- Analogous: This colorful theme uses colors next to each other on the color wheel, resulting in a harmonious color scheme often found in nature.

- Complementary: Here, colors opposite each other on the color wheel are combined, creating high contrast and a vibrancy perfect for highlighting specific elements in your animation.

- Split-Complementary: This scheme generates strong visual contrast while maintaining balance by using a base color and two colors adjacent to its complement.

## 5.2. Using Colors to Convey Emotion

Now that you have a fundamental understanding of color theory, let's delve into the link between color and emotion. As an animator, your color choices can make the viewers elated, restless, relaxed, or melancholic.

Analyzing your storyboard's key moments could help choose the right color schemes that evoke the intended emotions. For example, a scene depicting a character's joy could benefit from a warm color scheme, while a moment of suspense or mystery can adopt a cooler palette of blues and greens.

## 5.3. Color in Character Design

In character design, your choice of color can reflect personalities and backstories. Princess Elsa from Frozen is undoubtedly associated with an icy blue, reflective of her powers, while Shrek's unique green shade separates him from the usual fairytale creatures.

Test your characters under different lighting scenarios to ensure consistency with their color palette. Always note the color psychology behind your choices. Methodical selection can turn these characters into recognizable icons for your young audience.

## 5.4. Color in Background Design

Background color selections set the animation's environment and ambiance. They frame the narrative and assist in steering and augmenting the viewer's emotional connection with the drama unfolding within each scene.

Seasons can bring about different color inspirations. A spring vibe could embrace a fresh, vibrant palette, with lush greens and flower hues, while a winter theme could display cool, muted blues and whites, evoking feelings of tranquility or isolation.

## 5.5. Stylizing Your Animation with Color Themes

With your color theory in place, evoking accurate emotions and creating iconic characters, you can adopt unique color themes or styles that can become synonymous with your animation.

Pixel art style uses bold, bright colors and offers a retro aesthetic. Monochromatic style, favoring one base color across different hues for a timeless, classic feel, could be a chosen style. Watercolor-inspired styles lend a soft, dreamy, and fluid appearance to the animation. Identifying your animation's unique visual theme and sticking to it translates into a consistent viewing experience.

## 5.6. Color: A Powerful Storytelling Tool

Finally, remember that effective use of color can turn your animation from ordinary to remarkable or from simplistic to profound. Embrace color as a crucial storytelling tool—use it to convey mood, depict time and weather, emphasize important elements, signal character transformations, and capture your young viewers' imaginations.

Understanding the science and psychology of colors is one of the first steps into the magical journey of creating your animated world. Let's not just make animations, let's 'paint' animations and breathe unique life into every frame. As we nurture young creators, we hope this understanding of color will form a strong foundation and inspire them to explore, experiment, and express their creativity in the spectrum of their storytelling.

# Chapter 6. Creating Characters: Imagination Meets Digital Canvas

Let's begin an enchanting journey, where wild imaginings shape themselves into digital existence. Capturing the essence of your child's inventive characters onto a digital canvas involves both creativity and technique alike.

## 6.1. The Basics: Character Sketching

Creating the basic shape of your character is the first step in this magical process. It involves sketching out a simple structure that represents the character. Start with geometric figures to represent the different parts of the body, using circles for the head and body, rectangles for arms and legs, and smaller circles for joints. Make sure to maintain the proportionality of each part in relation to the others for a believable look.

Stylize these shapes to align with the character's personality. For example, a strong, muscular character might have broad, roughly rectangular upper body shapes, while a delicate or nimble character may have more slender, softly rounded shapes.

Remember, these shapes are just the beginning. Their purpose is to provide a solid base on which to build your character. They'll eventually be transformed with more intricate details like clothing, hair, and facial features.

## 6.2. Faces and Expressions: Mirror to Emotions

No character is complete without a face that expresses emotions. To begin, divide your character's head shape (usually a circle or an oval) into halves, both horizontally and vertically. The intersection would mark the placement of the nose, with eyes sitting along the horizontal line, and the mouth below the nose. Don't forget to adjust this basic structure as per your character's dimensions and shapes.

To express emotions, focus on the eyes and mouth. Play with their shapes and sizes, adjusting the eyebrows, and curvature of the mouth according to the emotion you wish to capture. Practice drawing faces expressing a range of feelings like happiness, anger, surprise, sadness, and more, to breathe life into your characters.

## 6.3. Outfits and Accessories: Reflecting Personality

Often, characters are recognized by their iconic clothing or accessories. These elements can reflect their character traits, history, or role in the story. When designing these, let your imagination take the reins. Take inspiration from real-world fashion trends, historical periods, or futuristic styles.

Remember to match these elements to the character's personality and functionality. A superhero may need a cape or a suit, while a pirate might don a tricorn hat and an eye-patch. Create a few variations, and decide on an outfit and a couple of key accessories that best support the character's identity and the story.

# 6.4. Colors and Textures: Framing the Mood

Color and texture play a powerful role in storytelling, often setting the tone or mood of scenes. When bringing your characters to life, consider what colors and textures best represent them.

Are they warm and inviting? Maybe go with soft, warm colors. Are they mysterious and elusive? Possibly cooler hues and jagged textures could work. Each color carries different emotional connotations, and textures can add another layer to the visual narrative of the character. Don't forget to experiment with shading and gradients to give a sense of depth and three-dimensionality.

# 6.5. Character Movements: Adding the Spark

Animating your characters is where the real fun begins. Start by understanding the basics of a walking cycle, an essential part of any animation. A basic walking cycle involves movement of legs and arms in contrasting directions- when the right arm moves forward, the left leg moves forward and vice versa.

To add further depth, incorporate facial expressions and body language into movements. The manner in which a character moves can contribute greatly to their personality. Is your character energetic, with quick, buoyant movements, or more relaxed and languid with slow, graceful gestures?

A good practice would be studying real-life movements. Understand how different emotions can make us move differently. This will bring a realistic touch to your animations.

# 6.6. Digital Tools: Bringing It All Together

Now that you've a clearer understanding of character creation, it's time to translate all that onto our digital canvas. There are several softwares available - both free and paid, such as Pencil2D, Blender, or Adobe Animator, which you can use according to your comfort and requirements.

When choosing your tool, consider factors like user interface, available features, and compatibility with your device. Begin with beginner-friendly tools with intuitive interfaces before moving on to more complex ones.

Software tutorials can help you navigate through the different options and features, ensuring you get the most out of your chosen tool. Be patient with your progress as digital tools require time to understand and effectively use.

From this magical art of character creation, your young ones not only learn to create vibrant characters from their imagination but also understand the emotions and movements that give them depth and life. Most importantly, their unique creations will endow them with an invaluable sense of achievement and creative satisfaction.

# Chapter 7. Dynamics of Motion: Animating Your Characters

Your child's characters are not merely static drawings, they need to move and interact with the world around them. That is where the magic of animation shines, and the dynamics of motion play a critical role. It adds life, emotion, context, and continuity to the narrative. This chapter will guide you through the essential concepts of motion dynamics, its significance, the techniques to master it, and some hands-on exercises.

## 7.1. Understanding The Dynamics of Motion

Decoding the dynamics of motion means understanding how things move. In animation, this concept of motion is central. It's not simply about making your characters move: it's about infusing them with the essence of life. Realistic motion demands a deep understanding of physics and kinetic principles, which may seem complex, but don't worry, we'll break it down in simpler terms.

The first step is observing. Encourage your child to closely study how their pets move or how trees dance in the wind. These observations lay the foundation for understanding motion dynamics. Digital animation isn't confined to realism, but a basic sense of real-world motion helps in creating convincing animations.

# 7.2. From Still Drawings to Moving Pictures

The basic premise of animation is to create an illusion of movement. This is achieved using a series of images, each one slightly different from the last. When these images are displayed quickly, it creates the perception of movement, like a flipbook.

In digital animation, these individual images are called 'frames', and an animation clip comprises numerous frames played in sequence. The speed at which these frames change contributes to the overall feel of the movement - a faster change means speedier motion, and a slower change means slower movement.

# 7.3. Mastering Keyframes

'Keyframes' are critical in the animation process. They are the significant points in the time frame where the motion changes direction or speed or both. For example, in a jumping sequence, the keyframes could be when the character is standing, bending to jump, at the highest point of the jump, landing, and standing again. A computer animation program uses these keyframes to calculate and fill in the frames in between - a process known as 'tweening'. Understanding and mastering keyframes are crucial to successfully animating characters.

# 7.4. Principles of Animation

Credited to Disney's pioneer animators, the 12 principles of animation lay firm guidelines for creating engaging and lifelike animations. Here are a few critical ones:

*Arcs: Natural actions tend to follow an arched trajectory, and animation should adhere to this principle as well. An arced path adds to the natural look and feel in animation.*

Overlap and Follow Through: Parts of a character can move at different rates. For instance, if a dog starts running, the body may lead the motion, with the tail following.

# 7.5. Hands-on Practices

*Guided Exercise - Walk Cycle: A walk cycle is a great animation to start with. It's a looping sequence which means that the start and the end frames are identical, and are connected seamlessly to create the illusion of a continuous walk.*

DIY Exercise - Jump Sequence: A jump sequence lets your child understand how to apply the principle of 'Anticipation', 'Follow through' and 'Arcs'. Encourage them to sketch key poses and fill the in-between frames.

Let Your Imagination Run Wild: Animation is all about creativity. After guiding your children with basic exercises, let them create a simple story with motion. This could be a bird flying, a cat chasing a mouse, or even an apple falling from a tree.

Remember: Practice makes perfect. Encouraging your children to practice different sequences and animate stories will help them get the hang of the exercises and master the motion dynamics.

# 7.6. Software for Kids

In the digital age, there are plenty of animation software available that are kid-friendly. Some popular options include Krita, Pencil2D, Tux Paint, Scratch, MS Paint, etc. All these platforms offer intuitive interfaces and tools that make it easy for kids to experiment with animation.

Following these guidelines and exploring the dynamics of motion, your journey in the realm of digital animation is sure to be epic, mesmerizing, and filled with fun. As our young creators enjoy telling and animating their tales, each stroke, each frame, each character, and each motion becomes an exploration of endless creativity.

# Chapter 8. Setting the Scene: Crafting Engaging Backgrounds

To make an astounding animation, the first and foremost step is crafting a scene, a setting that will host your story. It's not just about having characters; backgrounds are a vital part of your animated story, as they establish the mood, context, and place of action. They become characters in their own right, narrating a silent yet influential part of your story. It is the unsung supporting actor, adding depth, enhancing narratives, and aiding your character's emotions effectively.

## 8.1. Understanding The Importance of Backgrounds

Backgrounds are like the soul of your animated story. It's the environment where your characters will exist, interact, and relay their narratives. It gives your audience a sense of space and time and forms the essential frame of reference for the on-screen action.

Recognizing the crucial role of backgrounds can make an immense difference in how you approach animation. Your young one can utilize backgrounds to their advantage, employing them as a tool to describe, amplify, and support their narrative. It wouldn't be an exaggeration to say that a well-designed background can spell the difference between a flat, monotone animation and one teeming with life and energy.

# 8.2. Elements To Consider While Creating Backgrounds

Before we delve into the techniques of creating backgrounds, let's explore the essential elements you should consider while designing them.

## 8.2.1. Color

Color plays an instrumental role in setting the mood of a scene. Warm colors like red, orange, or yellow can reflect happiness, energy, or excitement, while cool colors like blue or green induce feelings of tranquility or sadness. It contains the power to evoke significant emotional reactions in the viewer, directly impacting how they feel about the scene.

## 8.2.2. Perspective

Perspective sets the groundwork for a three-dimensional illusion on a two-dimensional surface, providing depth to your scene. Neglecting perspective can result in a flat, unrealistic background.

## 8.2.3. Detailing

Detailing can make your backgrounds look more realistic or whimsical, depending upon the style of your animation. However, it's important not to overpower your main characters. Remember that your background should support and not steal the show.

## 8.2.4. Lighting

Lighting can have a dramatic effect on your backgrounds, lending depth, mood, and realism. Different types of lighting can evoke different emotional responses from your viewers.

## 8.3. Starting With Sketches

Before finalizing your background, sketch multiple drafts. This is an excellent way to explore different ideas, perspectives, and color schemes. Encourage your young one not to worry about the details in this stage; it's more important to get the ideas flowing.

List checklist items for sketching backgrounds: - Rough drafts of different perspectives. - Trying out various color schemes. - Brainstorming on the mood of the scene using light and shadow. - Visualizing how characters would interact with the backdrop.

Once you have a draft that you're satisfied with, proceed to refine it. Introduce more details into your sketch, correct any uneven lines, and perfect your perspective.

## 8.4. Incorporating Color In Your Backgrounds

Post sketching, one of the defining elements to furnish your scenes with is color. As mentioned before, colors can set the mood for your scene. While choosing colors, consider the time (day/night), weather conditions, and the feelings you wish to evoke in your viewers. A sunset scene could utilize warm hues, likewise, for a gloomy mood, perhaps opt for darker shades.

## 8.5. Utilizing Perspective

The principle of using perspective in your animation can be introduced to your young creators in a simple and fun way. By using the approach of one-point or two-point perspectives, an illusion of depth and three-dimensionality can be easily achieved.

### 8.5.1. One-Point Perspective

One-point perspective involves a single vanishing point located on the horizon line. Parallel lines like the sides of a road or long hall converge at this point, making objects appear smaller as they get further away.

### 8.5.2. Two-Point Perspective

Two-point perspective uses two vanishing points, typically on opposite ends of the horizon line. It's great for drawing objects at an angle rather than facing straight on or directly from the side.

# 8.6. The Role of Detailing and Lighting

With color and perspective sorted, your next steps are detailing and lighting. Remember, the key to detailing is balance – you want enough detail to make the background interesting, but not so much that it diverts attention from the main characters. Also, try to add elements that increase a scene's authenticity such as a clock on a wall or a tree in a park.

Once your details are in place, consider how lighting can enhance your scene. Light coming from different directions creates shadows, enhancing the authenticity and dramatic effect of your background. From backlighting to top lighting, each variation has its unique effect.

With these tools ready, your young animator can recreate any world they dream of. Make sure to remind them that while precision is important, it's essential that they enjoy the process of creating an animated world from scratch. After all, passion and joy in the act of creation are infectious, translating into the audience's reaction to their final animated masterpiece.

# Chapter 9. The Role of Music and Sounds: Igniting Emotions

Music and sounds serve a pivotal function in the realm of digital animation, coloring our imagined worlds and evoking emotions in a manner that visual imagery alone cannot achieve. What would 'Star Wars' be without John Williams' stirring score or 'Wall-E' without sound designer Ben Burtt's evocative noisescape? Sounds and music give voice to silent screens and are integral in creating immersive, animated experiences for our young creators and their audiences.

## 9.1. The Symphony of Stories

Unlike live-action filming, animations are created in a silent vacuum where every sound, every note, has to be thoughtfully added. This is where the role of sound design comes into play - an invisible hand that guides the emotional course of a story.

In movies, when a character slides, it's just recorded, but for animation, the sound has to be created from scratch, often using unlikely sources. Have you ever noticed the odd-intriguing 'swoosh' when Spiderman shoots out a web? It's actually the sound of a sticky tape roll being undone - a testament to the creativity involved in sound design.

The art of mapping stories with apropos sound is engaging, isn't it? Well, here are a few tips to get your children started. First, encourage them to pay attention to the sounds around them. A dripping tap, a car engine, the rustling of leaves - everything can be used to fabricate a stunning soundscape.

# 9.2. Sound Effects: The Aura of Animation

In animation, sound effects provide a sense of reality to the visually thrilling, but initially silent, world. They pave the way for an authentic experience, defining the on-screen activities. From the simple 'whoosh' of an object to the complicated growling of a creature, sound effects mark the presence and actions of characters, making them come alive.

One of the simplest ways to experiment with sound effects is using objects around your house. A heavy book being thumped shut can stand for a door closing, the crumpling of aluminum foils can replicate fire, or shaking a box of pasta can emulate rain. Let your children experiment and explore the endless possibilities.

# 9.3. Music: Melodies and Motifs

Next to sound effects stands the monumental role of music - the emotional underlining of every story told via animation.

Think of it as the voice of the silent protagonist, the atmospheric soul of the narrative. It can induce laughter in a comedy scene, create tension during a thrilling chase, or drench viewers in nostalgia within a remembering sequence. These melodies and motifs help in establishing characters, dramatizing situations, and indicating transformations.

To get started on composing music, kids can use a keyboard or software like GarageBand, which has a vast library of instruments and sounds. They can make their animations more moving by exploring major (happy) and minor (sad) scales, upbeat tempos for energetic scenes, and slow ones for more contemplative moments.

# 9.4. Foleys: The Footsteps of Realism

Foley artists create many of the sounds we associate with actions in animated films. Named after sound-effects artist Jack Foley, these sounds, like footsteps or rustling clothes, amplify the realism of characters. Creating 'Foleys' is an excellent activity for your children - a fun and engaging way to make their animations feel more real.

Guide them in recording sounds created by simple activities like walking, clapping, or slamming a door shut. Remember, the key is in the details. The crunch of snow underfoot will require a different effect than walking on a gravel path.

# 9.5. The Final Mix: Completing the Soundscape

After building a library of sounds effects, music, and Foleys, the final step is to mix these components together competently. This process is about balancing the various elements to ensure that crucial moments or dialogue aren't drowned out by overpowering music or sound effects.

Programs such as Audacity or Adobe Audition serve as great starting points for young learners to experiment with mixing sounds. Your kids can start with simple scenes, gradually moving to more complex arrangements as they grow comfortable with the process.

Before we finish, let's remember that creating sound design for animations is not only about using software and tools. It's all about letting your imagination run wild. So, let your children listen to the world around them and, equipped with these secrets, set off on their animated adventure to animate not just with colors, but also with sounds that truly make their stories come alive.

The power of sounds and music cannot be underestimated, as it breathes life into the animated narrative, lending it depth, dimension, and dynamism. In animation, as in life, it's the unspoken element that often makes the loudest statement.

# Chapter 10. Editing and Polishing: Fine-tuning Your Animated Story

In the grand spectrum of animation creation, editing and polishing is a stage that demands painstaking attention. It's a lot like refining raw gold, transforming it into something of intricate beauty and grandeur.

## 10.1. The Art of Editing

Believe it or not, editing isn't solely about cutting, trimming, and toying around with different scenes. It's an art that breathes life into the raw footage, basking it in the emotions you intend to convey. Remember that a well-edited story is often the one most remembered.

To get started, open your animation software and import your scenes. Early on, don't worry too much about specific timing or transitions. Your initial focus should be on getting the scenes in the correct order, laying down the basic structure of your story.

Additionally, consider the pace of your animation. Fast-paced isn't always better. Slowing down can be effective in capturing emotion and building suspense. This is where the magic of editing truly shines; it gives rhythm to your story, like a carefully composed piece of music.

## 10.2. Adding Transitions

Once you're satisfied with the order of your scenes, start intensifying your storytelling by adding transitions. There are many types to utilize such as Fade In, Fade Out, Cross Fade, Wipe, Slide, and more.

When correctly used, transitions can:

- Establish time passage
- Link together two related scenes
- Indicate a change in location
- Soften the jump between two drastically different scenes

However, remember that the key is balance. Too many dramatic transitions can distract from your story rather than enhance it. Often, a simple cut is the most effective transition for a seamless flow.

# 10.3. Sound Editing

Animation without sound is like a body without a soul. Background music, sound effects, and voiceovers together create a sonic landscape that further immerses your audience in the story.

Adjust the volume of your tracks so that one doesn't drown out another. For voiceovers, ensure the voices are clear and not overshadowed by the background music or sound effects. Balance is everything.

Next, experiment with different sound effects. Many animation software tools come with libraries of royalty-free sound effects. From the sound of a rushing river to the chirping of birds, and to the hushed whispers of the wind, effects give depth to the animation.

Don't forget the role of silence. As with visual transitions, breaks in audio can denote shifts or evoke certain emotions.

# 10.4. Improving Visuals

At this stage, strengthen your animation's visual appeal using color correction, filters, and effects. Correction is not just about fixing errors; it also involves enhancing visual quality or creating a unique aesthetic.

Think about bigger elements like brightness, contrast, saturation, and hue. Then look to smaller details like the variants of shadows, highlights, and mid-tones of different colors. A slight tweak can create a huge impact, for instance, desaturating colors can suggest a somber or nostalgic mood.

Certain animation software also provides options to add special effects. Ranging from sparkles and shadows to blurs and beams, various effects can enhance the visual narrative.

# 10.5. Polishing Animation

Polishing is the final process, almost microscopic tweaks that really differentiate a professional piece of work from an amateur one.

Keep an eye out for rough edges in the transition and movement of objects. Also, pay attention to the 'arcs' of movements. In real life, most movements follow a somewhat curved path rather than a straight line, and maintaining these arcs makes for a natural-looking animation.

Then, focus on timing and spacing. Timing refers to the number of frames for a particular movement, while spacing denotes the placement of those frames. Proper timing and spacing add weight and believability to the motion.

Lastly, review your entire animation for quality and consistency. It could be a question of visual effects and transitions, a matter of color themes and style, or an examination of sound and dialogue. It's time to smoothen out all discrepancies and unify the piece into a coherent whole.

Creating an animation is a meticulous journey echoing sentiments of passion, patience, and practice. As you tread along the path, remember the beauty of storytelling lies in the journey rather than the destination. The various stages of editing and polishing are but stepping stones that pave the way to your animated masterpiece. Now, breathe life into your narrative, sprinkle magic into the visuals, and craft a symphony of sounds. The world is ready to be mesmerized by your story! Happy Animating!

# Chapter 11. Sharing Your Masterpiece: Platforms and Social Media

Now that your child has given form to their imagination and created their splendid animation, the next exciting step is to share their masterpiece with the world. Here, we unveil various platforms and social media channels that are available - discussing their features, pros and cons, and guidelines to sail through these digital seas successfully.

## 11.1. Understanding Platforms

An important aspect before sharing your animations is to understand the different digital platforms available. The choice of platform depends on several factors including the target audience, content, and personal preferences. Here, we touch upon some popular ones:

1. YouTube: This video sharing giant needs no introduction. With over 2 billion monthly users, it offers a wide reach. Primarily meant for a general audience, having a channel dedicated to your animations can be beneficial.

2. Vimeo: A community-powered video sharing platform. Unlike YouTube, Vimeo focuses on high-quality, creative content, which can result in better visibility for unique animations.

3. Instagram: A platform where visuals take center stage. With its features like IGTV, Instagram Stories, and Reels, it's a great place for an artist to showcase short, snappy animations.

## 11.2. Setting Up Your Channel

Once you've decided on the platform, setting up your channel is crucial. Name the channel something that resonates with the animations' theme. Create a catchy, description that effectively conveys what your content is about. Adding meaningful tags can improve searchability.

## 11.3. Preparing the Animation for Upload

This process includes multiple steps to ensure the animation is in the optimal format for viewing online:

1. Rendering the Animation: File formats differ from platform to platform. For instance, YouTube accepts most video formats, Vimeo prefers MP4, while Instagram supports MP4 and MOV.

2. Final Checks: Play the animation completely to ensure there are no glitches or mistakes.

3. Thumbnails and Titles: A catchy title and interesting thumbnail are crucial for attracting viewers.

## 11.4. Sharing on Social Media

Now, let's explore sharing through social media. Use social media to tease your content, engage with your audience, and share updates. Facebook, Instagram, Twitter, and Pinterest are some of the platforms that can showcase your animations.

1. Teaser Content: Teasers build anticipation. Post a short clip or image from the animation, creating intrigue about what's coming next.

2. Regular Updates: Posting regularly helps retain audience interest.

3. Engaging with Your Audience: Respond to comments and messages. Encourage feedback and suggestions.

## 11.5. Social Media Etiquette

Though it's exhilarating to share animations, social media etiquette is a must. Respect others' opinions, avoid spamming, credit your sources, and always keep in mind the age-restriction guidelines.

## 11.6. Protecting Your Work

Watermark your animations, or use mechanisms like digital signatures to safeguard your creations. Copyright laws vary by country, so it's essential to familiarize yourself with the pertinent laws in your region.

## 11.7. Analytics & Feedback

Understanding analysis reports can help improve the visibility and reach of your animations. Feedback from viewers is also a rewarding way of improving the quality and content of your animations.

## 11.8. In Conclusion

Sharing animations is more than just showcasing your work. It is about community building as well. Although the process can seem overwhelming, this journey of sharing can be a joyous, inspiring, and educational endeavor.

Always remember, every animation you and your child create and share is a wonderful journey of learning, expression, and joy. It is a chance for your child's creativity to shine, narrate stories and create worlds that entertain, inspire, and bring smiles to faces around the globe.